ZACHARIAH AND THE POPPY LADY

A Story about Memorial Day

Written by Ellen Everly

Illustrated by Jeff Sims and Emma Riehlman

Copyright © 2016 by Ellen Everly

Zachariah and The Poppy Lady
A Story About Memorial Day
by Ellen Everly

Printed in the United States of America.

ISBN 9781498480581

All rights reserved solely by the author. The author guarantees all contents are original and do not infringe upon the legal rights of any other person or work. No part of this book may be reproduced in any form without the permission of the author. The views expressed in this book are not necessarily those of the publisher.

www.xulonpress.com

In Flanders Fields

In Flanders fields the poppies blow
Between the crosses, row on row,
That mark our place; and in the sky
The larks, still bravely singing, fly
Scarce heard amid the guns below.

We are the Dead. Short days ago
We lived, felt dawn, saw sunset glow,
Loved, and were loved, and now we lie
In Flanders fields.

Take up our quarrel with the foe:
To you from failing hands we throw
The torch; be yours to hold it high.
If ye break faith with us who die
We shall not sleep, though poppies grow
In Flanders fields.

DEDICATION

THIS BOOK IS DEDICATED TO <u>ALL</u> MEN AND WOMEN WHO HAVE FOUGHT TO GIVE US THE FREEDOMS WE ENJOY IN THIS COUNTRY.

*ACKNOWLEDGMENTS: Untold thanks to **Jeff Sims**, fellow teacher, for illustrating this book and doing the research to find the grave marker of an area veteran. Thanks to **Emma Riehlman**, student, for putting color into the illustrations. Many thanks, also, to **Zachary Olmsted**, student, and his mom for the effort necessary for Zach to be the boy model. Many, many thanks to **Theresa Zupan**, veteran, for her encouragement and counsel. The Poppy lady character was modeled after Mrs. Zupan and will serve as a memorial to her.*

It was Saturday and Zachariah and his father were going to the grocery store as they did every weekend while Zach's mom slept in.

The sun was already bright in the clear blue sky and Zach was excited about the trip to the playground which he and his dad would take after they picked up donuts at the store.

But something was different today. Next to the usual flowers and potting soil which were outside the store, there was a woman dressed in an odd-looking uniform. In front of her were some coffee cans. One seemed to be empty, but the other held some unusual flowers.

Zach was curious about everything so he asked his dad about the old woman. "Why don't you ask her," his dad suggested quietly. Giving his father a nervous glance, Zach stepped a little closer to the woman. "What are you doing?" Zach asked as respectfully as he could.

Slowly the old woman knelt down to speak to Zach. "Do you know about soldiers, Young Man?" Her voice was slow, but soft and it made Zach a little less nervous. "Of course, I do! They fight people who want to make the world a worse place," said Zach.

"Yes, and sometimes they die," replied the old woman. Zach was very surprised because most people didn't talk to kids about dying. He knew this because his grandfather had died last year and no one wanted to talk with him about it.

"Do you know about Memorial Day?" asked the old woman.

"Sure, we learn about it in school and we go to a big parade!"

Very quietly this time, the old woman asked another question. "Do you know what Memorial Day is for?"

The woman was so serious that Zach stopped smiling about the parade with the music, balloons, fire trucks, and CANDY, lots of candy. He thought a minute, remembered there were also men wearing uniforms sort of like the one the woman was wearing and then said, "I guess it's to remember… the soldiers."

"Yes, it is. And it is also when people go to the cemetery to decorate the graves of soldiers. They put flowers and flags on the graves to show that they are thankful to the soldiers. It used to be called Decoration Day. But sometimes," the old woman continued, "people forget that soldiers have died so they can be free." Zach knew he would never forget his grandfather and he thought it was sad that anyone would be forgotten.

"So," the old woman continued in her soft voice, "I collect money to help the soldiers who did not die by selling these flowers to help people remember. Would you like to wear a flower to help people remember the soldiers?"

Zach looked eagerly up at his dad. There was a big question in his eyes. Dad smiled and reminded Zach that he had money in his pocket. He could buy a flower himself.

Zach reached into his pocket and counted out his money. He shook his head. "No, Dad, I'm saving my money for something special. Could you buy the flower?"

"These are poppies," the old woman explained as Dad bought one for Zach and one for himself. Zach and his dad pinned the poppy stems onto their shirts, said thank you to the Poppy Lady, and continued on their trip into the grocery store.

A bit later, the Poppy Lady looked up to see them leaving the store. She expected to see Zach with a big, fat donut, but as she raised her hand to wave, she noticed that Zach was carrying an armload of flowers.

"Mmmm…," thought the Poppy Lady, "I wonder where he's going with those flowers?"

CPSIA information can be obtained
at www.ICGtesting.com
Printed in the USA
BVOW07s2252250816
460198BV00004B/34/P